SO-BDA-076

4

Publication of this book was made possible by a generous grant
from the Greenwall Fund of The Academy of American Poets.

This book is dedicated to
the memory of Andrew Jacob Fried

and to Damon Tomblin and Lizzette Potthoff

NOELLE KOCOT

FOUR WAY BOOKS
NEW YORK

Editorial Office
Four Way Books
PO Box 535
Village Station
New York, NY 10014

Library of Congress
Catalog Card Number: 00 134379

ISBN 1-884800-32-7

Book Design: Brunel

This book is manufactured in the United States of America and
printed on acid-free paper.

Four Way Books is a division of Friends of Writers, Inc.,
a Vermont-based not-for-profit organization.
We are grateful for the assistance we receive from individual
donors and private foundations.

ACKNOWLEDGMENTS

Grateful acknowledgment is made to the following publications:

6500: "Blood Brother"
The American Poetry Review: "Bad Aliens," "Last Words," "The Laugh of
    the Medusa," "Love Poem on the Anniversary of Nowhere," "Nostalgia,"
    "Signs of Life," "Why I Wish I Had Never Taken a Poetry Workshop"
Another Chicago Magazine: "Dasein"
Anodyne: "Abortion Elegy"
The Cape Rock: "Words and Things"
The Chattahoochee Review: "The Number 4 Comforts a Sad Child"
Conduit: "Brooklyn Sestina," "In Spring," "Outing," "What I Mean When
    I Say I'm a Poet"
Fence: "A Losing War," "Conversation at 5 O'Clock," "Hindsight Is Always
    Best," "Repeat After Me"
The Iowa Review: "Good Things Come to Those Who Wait," "Sestina
    for Lizzette"
Lilliput Review: "Sappho to Erinna"
Lit: "Bicycle Poem," "The Traffic Cop"
LUNGFULL!: "Bisexuality"
New American Writing: "Le Marteau sans maitre," "Ontology Train,"
    "The Passion According to G.H.," "Tribute"
Passages North: "An Ordinary Evening"
Rain City Review: "Having a Job," "Reconciliation," "What I Want to Tell
    You but Can't"

The poem "The Laugh of the Medusa" received the first annual
S.J. Marks Prize from *The American Poetry Review* for a poet's first
appearance in that magazine.

Many of these poems have been reprinted in the magazine *Survivorship.*

The epigraph that begins the book is an untitled poem taken from *Crow
With No Mouth: Ikkyū,* translated by Stephen Berg, published by Copper
Canyon Press.

In the poem "Good Things Come to Those Who Wait," the epigraph is
taken from "Questions of Travel" from *Complete Poems 1927-1979* by
Elizabeth Bishop, published by Farrar, Strauss, and Giroux.

In the poem "Dasein," the epigraph is taken from "Letter on Humanism" by Martin Heidegger in *Basic Writings,* ed. David Farrell, published by Routledge & Kegan Paul.

In the poem "Sestina for Lizette," the quote "a simple garden with acres of sky" is taken from the song "Into White" by Cat Stevens, on the album *Tea for the Tillerman,* on the Universal/A&M label.

The epigraph that begins section three is taken from the poem "Notes Toward a Supreme Fiction" from *The Palm at the End of the Mind: Complete Poems and a Play* by Wallace Stevens, published by Vintage Books.

In the poem "Le Marteau sans maitre," the title is taken from the poem of the same title by René Char.

In the poem "Repeat After Me," the quote "Who can say what it means or whether it protects?" is taken from the poem "Shadow Train" from *Shadow Train* by John Ashbery, published by Penguin Books.

In the poem "Repeat After Me," the quote "In the Middle of the Road" is taken from the song "Middle of the Road" by The Pretenders, on the album *Learning to Crawl*, on the Warner Brothers label.

In the poem "The Passion According to G.H.," "Lemonade, everything was so infinite" were Franz Kafka's last words as quoted in *The Hélène Cixous Reader*, ed. Susan Farrell, published by Routledge.

Grateful acknowledgement is made to the following people for their generous support: Brenda Hillman, Damon Tomblin, Denise Duhamel, Franz Wright, Jeannine Savard, Joanna Fuhrman, Joe Juracek, Joshua Clover, Lou Asekoff, Lizzette Potthoff, Nick Carbo, Norman Dubie, Rebecca Reilly, Sidney Wade, Steve Berg, Stuart Friebert, Tim Liu, William Logan, Zen Mountains and Rivers Order.

Many of the poems in this manuscript are addressed to specific individuals. Some of them are: "Good Things Come to Those Who Wait" for Alex Halberstadt, "Bad Aliens" for James Tate, "Tribute" and "Signs of Life" for Damon Tomblin, "Brooklyn Sestina" for Denise Duhamel, "Le Marteau sans maitre" for Mel New and "Having a Job" for Matt Rohrer.

CONTENTS

I

II

III

Much dreaming and many words are meaningless.
Therefore stand in awe of God.

—Eccles 5:7

You me when I think really think about it are the same

—Ikkyū

I

Good Things Come to Those Who Wait

Oh, must we dream our dreams and have them, too?
—Elizabeth Bishop

A paper hat transmutes so easily into a paper boat,
But this doesn't mean that the boat is somehow inferior.
I was a child once.
I saw into the deep, blue interior

Of the number four, which is the Holy Spirit who makes
All things possible and all things matter.
All things I thought of then,
Even the letter

Q without the U behind it. And things just settled.
There was no need to hope
For any more, except maybe a cigarette, and the thing about cigarettes
Is that one after another, they're the same. Meanwhile, soap

Dissolves much more quickly than it did in 1970,
The year that embarrasses me most with its promise of tall,
Musky, balding Gordons and Dons, with orange, palm-tree expressions,
And *women* in short, pregnant dresses and ash-black falls.

It will take a freighter
Of Coppertone to tan them all. Somewhere a library still swells with bean-
Bag chairs and barefoot, dozing hippies too hooked
On Marx and Keynes to notice that Miss Breen

Has in fact been able to write her roommate (friend, I presume)
Into her will with little fuss from the family. Anyway, I hope I've seen
The last of those backwards
Fools, except of course for kind-eyed Miss Breen

And her companion, who are coming
This Thursday for a good, strong cup of German tea. Hopefully, that rag
Of a newspaper will give us something to talk about before
We sip. Wait a minute! I must buy some Black Flag

So that the roaches spare our Lorna Doones! O world,
In all my years of comprehension
I will never understand their synchronous, immediate
Flocking in bright formation, then halting suspension

Beneath the sink when I turn on the fluorescent, kitchen, warehouse-
Like, blaring light just before sun-up. The blue
Spirit that I once saw radiating out from everything, like a tourist
In a too-young country, has gone home. And yes, I love you,

Yes, if to love implies more guilt than one alone can harbor.
So come, the scenery
Is fine here. The wild blue light still crosses the mountains
Now and then, somewhere a number four sprouts through the rough greenery.

Love Poem on the Anniversary of Nowhere

The ground is failing in my memory.
This shade is deafening. A false story
Welds me to a space where I neither
Wash my hair, nor fold my clothes,

Nor speak, nor even breathe, and I ask myself,
What favor can you do for me
That you have not already done? For instance,
When I wrote my name in the datebooks of angels

And I did not care whether they were fallen,
You didn't say a word.
But I heard your crystal clanging
From afar and I knew you'd finally come

To doubt the bodiless fire of marvelous dark
Fading softly into nearest stars above us. You wept.
The leaves fell one, two, three, infinity,
And you, my stalled train bound for eternity,

Remain sunk into the burning snow that caps the evil
River pumping my heart across the empty edge of space,
Where an intermezzo sleep of shadows writhes
Lightly on the throbbing, failing ground.

Sappho to Erinna

Come. It's morning.
Let me brush the stars
From your hair.

An Ordinary Evening

There I go again shoving my wheelbarrow
Of pain across the filthy streets
Of the dimly-lit city. No one stops me,
No one says anything like, "Here let me,"

Or "Jeez, what a wonderful thing
You have there, do you know where
I can get a thing like that?"
Instead we trundle along,

My wheelbarrow and I, dodging
The strollers and shimmering cars
Which look beautiful under the orange
Streetlamps, and everyone seems as blessed

As a holy star, and I forget
My wheelbarrow for a moment,
As one might forget a warning
In a dream, and in my mind, I gather

Various items: A net crammed with the scales
Of invisible fish, the wind that passes,
Singing, and all of my widowed beliefs
Lost in a language full of storms,

And I remember just what makes my garlands
Of solitude sway like the sea
In front of a lighthouse.
Then, in the crisp rottedness

That lines the question marks of steam
Coiling out of the potholes
Which I manage to avoid for the most part,
I ponder my wheelbarrow, and all

Of its inner-meaning, which is far sweeter
When trembling on the lips of a stranger
At the end of a thin day
That sheds its shadows like a dress,

And tosses them into the flames of sunset
Blazing up from the gasoline
Shrouding the asphalt, setting
The whole sidereal sidewalk of trees on fire,

And while the others have already fled,
You and I remain caught
In this conflagration, yet I can say nothing
And only observe the melting scene

Flashing across your beatific eyes,
And it is there, only there
That I can finally bring myself to say,

"Yes, I think I would like some help
With this. Here you go."

Last Words

As the moving vehicle approaches,
Your eyelashes tap out in code
How we once tossed in the shadows
Of our worried days, unbeguiled

By the windswept motions
Of nimble flowers (hell,
What did they know of somnambulism
Or love?) and how we sighed

While the sun warmed our hair
And everything faded to an astonished,
Steady humming. We ate metaphorical
Tranquilizers by the dozen,

By the gazillion, in that time
When you and I wrestled across
The page of a younger poem,
Our restlessness blossoming

Like yellow sponge from underneath
Certain upholstery. And fate followed us,
Yes, but not like a madman brandishing
A razor, more like a bureaucrat

Who manages to turn everything
Dreary into a useful skill.
The sunrises clambered on,
Each one more tiresome than the last,

Their unnaturalness akin to the sheen
Rippling across a sheet of imitation suede.
And the river of life slogged on
Beneath us, bracketed by its narrow banks.

As the moving vehicle approaches,
I am astounded that I have time to consider
Such things, that such things
Reveal themselves to me at all,

Seeing as how they are not the things
We thought we held most dear,
And it is as if they stand as signposts
That mark how futile it was for us

To detour each of the sharp-edged scraps
Strewn across road after level road,
And how in the end it steered us head on

Into a suffocating angel choking on a wishbone
Behind the wheel of a runaway truck.

Bad Aliens

They're really here, spreading their ideas
Like vulture droppings, conniving to sow
Their brazen ontologies like bone-encrusted wheat
Along our field of vision yellowed like an almanac,

Stringing our thoughts into a syzygy,
Until we cannot move them and feel instinctively
That we never will. The few, the very few,
Who escape become spokespeople for our cause,

And although their identities remain unknown
To even them, surely they will turn a phrase
Or two that will make the bastards think again
Before they steal our fluids in the night,

Suck the breath from our livestock, tearing
Off their very flesh, leaving a metallic aroma
In the air as if from singed, mineral-soaked hair.
The world is becoming a giant crematorium

Before our eyes. Next thing you know,
It'll be your big toe shot up with morphine
At your family reunion,
It'll be your child slurping blood

At First Communion, it'll be a havoc
Of suburban cannibalism bursting into flames
At the mere suggestion of an accident.
Meanwhile, the flowers hang like open mouths

As we walk around relishing
Our wisdom of refracted light.
The neighbors lounge outside the warehouse playing cards
While inside the aliens are at it again,

Warning the boy strapped to the steel table
As in a dream that he will find his end
In a myriad of abandoned mines.
And no one will come to look for him,

And no one will even think to, because by then
All will have been erased, by then we will have forgotten
Him as we have forgotten
The name of the druggist's Seeing Eye dog.

And we'll go on with our house-painting,
And we'll go on with our affairs
Of negligence, and we'll go about with our heroics
Of tin foil, and all the while the aliens

Will be waiting for the perfect hour
To land on the non-referential velvet of our lawns,
Bending each blade of grass perfectly
To match the charred feathers of the baby chicks

Still lining the barn walls from two Easters ago
Where they probed our insides brilliantly
For signs of redemption and were satisfied.
The aliens are here,

Permanently confirmed to walk among us
And because they're here already,
There will be no possession, no redeemer
Yet to come. Instead, a triangle in the sky

Reflects the sober landscape, a reminder
That angles are the highest fate of form
Like the beaten metal of shell-cases stabbing
The corners of the pulpy world.

The imprints of their ships
Reveal a plastic sincerity, as if all along
They were only here to help, as if stealing
Our children, their faces plastered

Permanently onto milk cartons were an intergalactic feat
Worthy of a stellar bow. We know they hold
The inevitable ace, we know they wear
The hereditary apparel of extinct, misty grasses

Overgrowing the sepulchral cloth
Of the earth. We stand frozen before their badness,
We are a smoky restaurant full of soldiers
That can fly off the globe at any moment,

Leaving their beams to bisect our newest footprints
With the mockery of some season's malingering death.
The three-sided pyramid of the occipital
Can deflect only so much into geometry

Of our collective breath. I would gouge
Out the insides of this sleep so big,
I would start my own crusade if I thought I had a chance,
But they're *bad*, they're bad for *real*.

And in the word *Bad*, bordered by flashing air,
I see the wheat spin a numeral's fiery dance,
And this leaves me with two questions:

—Why all this irony?
—Are you enjoying the view?

The Traffic Cop

As always, I expected too much
From the siren's hexed scream,
And what it flies in the face of is lamentable,
Like baby birds in winter scrunched

Inside their fist-sized nests.
Today I made myself a list:
Hack a path through the winding river
Just outside of town,

Tend to a widow's irradiated garden,
Remember to love, oh, remember...
Enough. As usual, I'm reduced to giving
Hand signals, short of breath

Like a sword coughing through the air
In a single person's joust.
I don't know how to say what I'm becoming,
But it seems that every time

I consider lolling on the banks of the lake
Of infernal fire, the ice-cream truck
Toddles along, hauling its song,
The only music I can bring

Myself to listen to these days.
The truth is, I'm bored,
And conversations about why don't seem to help.
I'm getting older fast and none too carefully,

And my vocation has shown itself
To be the same as any obsession
And what it has to do with.
The more I think out loud or try to break

With the striations of the night
That go by like a fluid through a monumental crate,
The more I sense the waffling
Of a dismal perfection parceling itself out

Like a morning that peels itself in strips
From eyes like the hazy skin of grapes.
The truth is, there are no rules here,
No signs buried in the anaphoric sunrises

Pouring down as slow as the colloidal
Substance of your lives,
No direction to the rains swaying in the summer wind
Like abandoned clotheslines of another time.

Your brand of peace disgusts me, do you hear?
I am the fugitive who drives a stampede
Of aardvarks across your lawns.
I have come to tip your cows.

I have eaten of all your trees
And still you do not know.

Why I Wish I Had Never Taken a Poetry Workshop

The ruined insistence of words inscribed
In the flakes of rusted sun before my eyes
Hang in time and dangle like hungry infants
From a caryatid's lustrous arms. There is no more

Hope for them than for the strange
And subtle whistling that one hears outside
One's window late into the night and finally
Turns to see the whistler who disappears,

And takes the whistling, too, as if on cue.
Nevertheless, the features of the whistler progress
In unremembered dreams which diminish by half-lives.
If I had only stood still,

Waited in the slow strangulation of schoolmarm
Voices for the original word to sink,
A watery diamond through a river of felled trees,
To sink itself into the drowned aviary

Of my brain, perhaps I would not have propped myself
So readily upon the lamp-lit discourse pillowing my head
Into too much sleep. But alas, as is my habit,
I sped past them like an ostrich, with wax wings

To make it worse, stumbling and sputtering
Past the fleeting friction of seasons
Until I melted and deformed into a warped
Staircase wending its way up toward a fixed idea

That hung in vials of holy water from the necks
Of the Eumenides masquerading as a cloud.
If I could crumple all these thoughts
Into tiny balls of lead or leaves,

I would not be concerned at all with finding
Those fine balances ringed round with shame
Or pride, like an egg reduced to cracking
Because it cannot sustain itself even in the gentlest

Hand's stormy vise. But as I can fit
My thoughts into a coffee cup,
What else can I do but use this lassitude
As a mockery of the clear path's reflection

That enjoins me to forever walk on sunny streams?
Ever since I was a failed child, I've known
How reveries can be shattered into symbols
That I will never call by name,

How each man or woman can be worn
Like a holster by another man or woman's side.
I did not need to be reminded once again,
Did not need to hear,

"There's too much glittering starlight here
To see the glittering starlight."
I was already blind to diamonds, and to stars,
And the emptiness there was just exquisite

To my touch: Only the Braille embossed across the fire
That lit the coals beneath an ancient kettle whistling,
Keening like an infant through a night so songless,
And yet the embers danced.

Words and Things

The tiny acrobat
Of joy

Leaps the distances
We do not speak,

As if our tongues
Were as mangled

As the first cries
Of a newborn

Pouring into the sickle-
Grin of moon,

And hovers over
The net

Of the already-
Said and laughs

And laughs
Into that silence

While sun sinks
And we lie

Hammocked
And waiting

For tranquilized
Sleep

Nudging at one
Another and mumbling

About nothing
In particular.

Ontology Train

The abracadabra of midnight fields slipping past
At ruinous speed carries the same aqueous
Lassitude as a daylight moon in its last
Yellow dangling hour marking its exodus

With an angry rain. The night offers no apology
For its marvelous moody technique bathed in the venom
Of so many charged similes that conjure the hagiography
Of man as a vessel caught in a maelstrom

Which is his own blustery hubris pulsing
Through his homesick blood with an objectivity
As dry as the chill air rising
From the nostrils of a sleeping nativity.

The quest to make mystery something indivisible
Inflates the worship of the synthetic outlines
Etched solemnly around our figures grouped rigid
In pharaonic files along some spectral shrine

That holds the key for whoever will translate
Our majestic solitudes and thereby free us
From our mediocrity. Finally, we will be able to annotate
Our facile repetition, and this in turn will give new impetus

To plunge ourselves comet-like straight into adventure
Across a modulated sky as seen through drapes
Half-drawn across a double-glass window. The failure
Of optical laws until then in aiding our escape

Only confirms our penchant for contradiction,
Which is like a cork nestled in the interpenetrating crests of waves.
Our almost dancing steps betray an elation
Which gives way to anguish the moment we first crave

A secret intimacy with the spacious horizons
And the vast reaches of the sea. But the very concept
Of awe capsizes when one abandons
Oneself to a new rigor, consciously built on the contrast

Between our choreographic frolics and the sensory abundance
Of the landscape's thread of unbroken colors trailing off
With the spirited opulence
Of gold and precious stones. The rough

Disorder of our singularities, discontinuous, vague,
Washes over us once more before the blue, powdery film of day
Descends like hospital curtains over a quarantined plague
Whose stricken are more well-rehearsed than actors in a play.

Outing

You laughed furtively on the cliffs
As if our outing were nothing more
Than a great brown joke
In the toilet of oblivion.

The sky smeared banners all over the place.
There was a violent disagreement
And the stars detained us,
The dry grass of lamentation pleased us.

Back in the city a turnstile flamed all night.
A soul rose twice from its ranks.
We spoke of energy
And how we would like a world where everyone wins a prize.

Bill was out celebrating his life,
Draping the clouds with harmonies and instincts.
By day he stuffed shiny things into mailboxes.
We both agreed, he'd be better off dead.

We folded the keys in their velvet cloth.
Some lighterfluid was percolating on the stove.
I thought about smog
And what it could be in the hands of a master.

Tribute

Those slacks sure look nice on you.
How about soaking them in some vermouth
To shrink them even tighter?
And this startling panorama

Of morgues and medical waste
Should do the trick merely through osmosis
So that soon everyone will know
The honorable knave you were

Before you simply got up and left your incubator,
Before the cadaverous nurses had their chance
At a kind of pure defenestration.
It must get tiring, all of this breathing in and out.

In those other times when you and I
Stayed only in our kitchen,
I was able to catch cloudy things between my teeth.
Then the paramedics, blossoming from their ambulance

Came for you, you remember, natives of Hawaii, etc.
In fact, in much the same spirit
As Charles Martin Hall when he said
Of aluminum, "I'm going to go for that metal"

(Oberlin College, circa 1905), and he did,
It was there that we decided to throw our annual bash,
To romp around in the uncorked fizzle
Of another fermented year,

And transmit signals as risqué as the whine
Of priapic cats back and forth
To camouflage our loneliness.
But as the eruption of our summer hair began,

We learned to clamp down
Upon that metal thrill of opportunity,
To catch the abiding light
In dollops of breakfast cereal left by the door

To a warehouse in somebody's hometown,
To kiss the moon like a private grapefruit
While the spinachy rains fell down
Like netting from our secret sky.

So much is passionate between us;
Nonetheless, we maintain our separate
Hemispheres tucked into the carapaces
Of the days that manage to claw their way

To the surface time and time again.
What is left fulminates above us
Like vatic staves of music
Puckered into a reverie of sheer dimension.

And the translucent folds of skin
Draped from our aging bones,
And the toupéed mesmerization
Of our lovely afternoons:

They are what we are with their crisp scent
Of vermouth and freshly-laundered slacks.

II

I have taken the path of least resistance,
Forsaking the bright and snowy wood,
And giving no credence to the dance
Of a sawdust puppet on an ancient rood.

And if I have fallen, it was only once,
A long time ago at break of day
When I heard your voice by happenstance
Call out beyond the death of this passion play.

Signs of Life

Somehow the blank page comforts me tonight,
And I know this solace that I feel will carry me
Through to that blonde and golden light.
I feel also that I have an errand in this stiff-backed chair;

Forgive me if instead of carrying it out
I reveal to you that I am a skeleton
Lying down beneath the ground you walk on,
Cushioning the fall of a still-born

Onto a liturgical stage, I am the masked one
Who tarries at the Lord's tomb
Under starlight squeezed from tubes
Of hardening paint which fathom the mystery

Of that great pain. The fatal language
Of the spirit dangles from my neck
And navigates me over these softly curving paths
Past an alchemist's cave which harbors

The voluptuousness of forbidden words.
Forgive me if the rhapsody of my longings
Cry tears of lye on a scale of Lydian proportions,
Then splatter down into a fiery trail

Of seasons that leads me back to the vulgar
Things that trip in the vermin-studded wind.
All I ask is that you let me wait for you,
As our days are shorter now

Than they ever were before,
And that menacing fishhook of sadness
Hangs like a moon above a bird-infested sea.
Those lost herds of phantoms are coming home to roost,

Ignorant of their desires.
I do not think they will roam anymore.
Tonight the town seems especially hushed,
As if it were holding its breath for an inheritance

Of some dimension, but both you and I know
The baptism of the insider is a lettered feat,
And that all the gadgets gone awry
Have wedged themselves into the smiles of murderers

Picnicking on a midnight heap of grassy ashes.
And the errand has been canceled on account of rain,
The errand all along being the done day
Which would unfold before us anyway.

Bicycle Poem

There were cathedrals falling out of your eyes
And your arms were the handlebars
I held in an abbreviated dream of crushed petals
Strewn across the limpid avenues.

I said, "I have poems for you"
But my words were lost in the wind.
I said, "I love you"
And you drifted into sleep.

And so I said nothing and rode you in and out of the rooms
Where we had stretched the boundaries of the soul
Like an endless sheet
And I felt you waking up between my legs.

Dasein

The Dreadful has already happened
    —Martin Heidegger

When we are quiet,
Being reveals itself in cheap silverware
On a freshly-set kitchen table.
It is *this* fork, *this* spoon, *this* knife.
They shine in their mysterious essences
Even more after they are mangled in the sink disposal
As our utensils are prone to be
When we are hopelessly forgetful.
And we hate to hear them,
Love to hear them, clinking away,
Clanking uproariously, bending and twisting
So that we can almost hear the rippling screams
Of the mad hoards drowning out the ghosts
Of lepers at the St. Lazare.
Listening to myself say this,
I realize the feeling is much the same
As when you reveal to me
Your absolute drunken astonishment
With a world that let you be fucked so far
In your two-year-old ass with a metal crucifix
That you dispersed into the pieces
You finally want back after so many years
Of not having the faintest idea
About what it is to want.
And as with anyone else, you are
All the more real in pieces,
Each grasping, as well as illuminated by,
Some such transgression.
Hold them in your open hands,
But only for a moment.
Let them spill through your fingers like water,
Like mercury, like Being itself.
For now, do not ask what happened or why.
Ask only, "Where do I end?"
And "How should I begin?"

Often I remind you that I too have walked
In the land of dreams and have become real.
With this I say that reality is signified
Only by how far your soul is allowed
To fly into space.
Listen to what it brings back,
To what it is trying to tell you.

Nostalgia

I

Whatever the cobalt sky intends
Today, the small gabled shapes leaping
In reflection off your eyes
Allow the sun to bend
Its leaden winter rays
Around this short and twisted street
Until they thin to the peace of a single
Line that evening will delete.
And whether you stand in the sunlight
Or in the shade, you are always
The light of a gray day
Careening past a woolly tree,
With the same blind love
As the shadows grazing lightly on your hair,
Which is, after all, a kind of love.

II

While you continue to hide yourself away
In some hotel, this season spreads a tablecloth
Of newly-fallen snow covered
By an immemorial, telluric dust
Illuminated by the artificial rust
Of streetlamps that shepherd
Him or her to their respective subways
As you sanctify your place among the lost.
And you observe patiently as your twin
Concerns of shadow and the day elapse
To little more than a powder shed over all created things
From buildings sawing the night into slabs
Without apology, and somewhere you know
That neither they nor you have failed.

III

Tonight the skeletons of umbrellas
Wound in sheets of rain clatter
Outside the rows of houses echoing
Themselves to sleep. You seem to be following
Me again, cowled in the vaguely starlit dark,
Feckless monk, silent witness to the shattering
Of glass around my soul which was
To take its refuge in a sanctuary more stark
Than in that blue-black morning vapor
Pillowing your face as you slept and walked,
Walked and slept, until your resolution fell away.
For now, you have dug your grave in my breast,
And I cannot apologize, because I have taken
The terrible oath to discern among the forms
That what dies lives, what lives dies.

I Want Something of Yours for Comfort When I Sleep

Awake before the cupboard slams open.
These hours scrape by like snow shovels.
I have dreamed of you again.
Too late, you said, *for me, but not for you*,
With the folly of a train darkening
In the failing embers of winter.

So I went on, flapping through time like a saw
In the wind, or like a melting fist
Weaned on the hardy light of day,
While the fading of our modesties
Blossomed into a cancer on love's faulty tongue.
And now your hair flames brightly in my kitchen cups.

The End of November

The afternoon falls like a heavy adornment
Sculpted out of ice. The door swings on protesting
Hinges that catch the light, glinting feverishly
On the scores of shapes vibrating upwards.

And in this language, ill-suited to our latitudes,
I see your face float like a portrait
Doomed to inexorable ruin, already distant,
As if viewed through gauze.

You go alone like a hangman, through the twisting
Alleys, the straight avenues of maples.
You drift through the neon and the tinsel
And the syncopated rattle of the city

Amid the westering sun streaming through
The haze as if through a stained glass
Window, splashing onto the concrete
As if onto the marble floor of your tomb

Where your epitaph is scrawled anew
Each day in color and in light.
You seem hoarded by darkness,
A dark cypress that stabs the skyline,

Without remotely apologizing for the portents
Strung like disembodied numerals
Around your branches. I imagine you
Fifty years from now, torrential,

Soft features graven into gullies where the eye
Will trace the outpouring of a mind
That outraced its time, and your eyes,
Finally emptied of their images shifting

Like quick-growing weeds in the wind,
Will fill with the inscapes of pilgrim chants
Echoing off the Iron Age of war
To become a morning breeze

Tugging at your shutters from behind which ruined
Palaces rise dreamlike from an agitated sea,
A labyrinth of living history
That fulfills its hope in the swiftness

Of the one sailboat punctuating it,
And the sky having momentarily cleared
Will open out onto a nameless laughter
That extends forever and forever.

Conversation at 5 O'Clock

What is revealed as night slashes
At the halted gnaw of machines?

The ladders of air sway in the high shadows.

At times, an avid broom sweeps past
And dusts away what is already written in ashes.

Only then do the precious vowels,
The most turbid flowers of our being, evolve.

Brooklyn Sestina: June, 1975

How can I conjure the vividness of the plastic
Blue and orange chairs we'd slump
Into every morning before the tyranny of fractions,
Each afternoon after the sadism of lunch?
We'd just played "Boys against Girls,"
"Girls against Boys," slamming each other's small bodies

Into a schoolyard fence, as if to add to the body
Of what American feminism had become, its piles of plastic
Dolls dismembered like Bluebeard's wives, only this time by girls
Of single mothers slumped
Into plaid couches, too tired or too drunk to fix those cleanly cut-out lunches
Like the ones beamed into their living rooms through the Cyclopean fractal

Blue-rimmed eye of the cathode ray refracted
By those radio ballads that sent everybody
Who'd ever broken up to sobbing in their McDonald's Muzak lunches.
Why is it that everything smelled like plastic
As the yellow heatwave slumped
Against my salmon-colored building where the girls

Were jumping rope (the older girls
Skipping double Dutch)? Could it have been the fractious
Yentas looking on from sweaty beach chairs clumped
Together in the shade, their widowed bodies
Already melted and annealed to a tanned and cracking plastic?
The housewives who went on serving each other lunch

Like it would never end? I would soon be off to lunch
Myself at Jewish camp with a girl
My age named Rachel, offering her what I'd plastic-
Wrapped the night before, her six-year-old fractions
Of hands fumbling over my body
In return before our midday swim. No Cold War, no economic slump

Could touch us in that Brooklyn; Brooklyn, the word itself seems holy,
    a Cabalistic lunchbox
Yawning open for all the world to fathom its great plastic
Letters stretched bodiless
Across the level see-saw of the summer heat like the broken balloon of a girl's
Insides, her future a fractal-
Patterned leaf dangling from her family tree of dusty plastic.

And the shoulders on the bodies of the girls
Who hadn't been pinned to their beds at night slumped in the lunchroom
Nonetheless, its fractured spoons and forks still scattering across
    the dancefloor of my dreams, a threnody of plastic.

Bisexuality

The bars on these windows eke
Out the burglars of my dreams,
While the hooks of sprouts in Dixie cups
Get tangled in this Lenten season.

There is a radio message in this vehicle
Of light: "It must be established
That kissing people will only bring more germs
And more immeasurable verbs,"

And I am reminded of a time when all of life
Seemed a tiring reach, when the length of a tree's shadow
Was proportionate only to the swallowed seeds
In my own true rind.

Now I am left to chirping and knocking down nests
While the butterflies trapped in my mouth fly out.
But the ochre of my rapacity
Is beyond subtlety this spring:

My mouth of suns waxes your cornucopic breathing,
The letters of half-unspoken words plunge
Themselves into your brows,
And the rest of the particulars dim and glow

Over your egg-white fingertips,
As the bars of moonlight spread wide
Across our shadows struggling to bless these spaces
Where mice have carved their sleep.

These feelings when they come, come in droves.

Abortion Elegy

And there you were, emerging alone into the light,
A sort of halo, scattering despite
My fierce and silent request, too late
To defer to my bird's-eye hindsight

Sinking to eye-level now before the portrait
Of you I'll never see, ever. Yet you are concrete
Somehow; I know, I've heard your bee-like buzzing
In all the tiny leaves bursting from their sacs to greet

A magical universe, where everything grows, and sings
In harmony for we know not what. Everything
Grows, even you, my little one, and your sanctity
Is that of a dim and stormy summer evening

With its regard for all things temporary.
So go now, dear, and go with dignity
Into the stark, mid-winter air, which is your birthright.
May your sleep keep you as warm as a September tree.

Reconciliation

for my father, 1943-1986

I am older when I see you
In the blue of a schoolyard fence,
Thick with stars.
A lone bird on a wire cries.
When I go to you,
You crumble like buildings
In a dream, past my arms
And you fall light—
Nothing but sawdust all along.

There is no need to ask what happened.
And I don't want to hear why
Anymore from your mouth,
Trembling against the pavement
Like so many weeds.

You say something
And I bend down to hear.
Soon our names will sleep.
I nod and walk away
While your eyes close
Into the dry dry air.

For My Father the Poet

I look and look for you in the eyes of other men,
Go on singing under the spires of the city
And its symphony of iron like a knife through wax
While the evening raises its scarred wrists
Over the stained awning of the sky
And again I find myself without you.
I want to say, I have fed the young, changed the seasons,
Banged into the silken necks of giraffes
Craning over the deep night of the truly dead.
I want to tell you that I carry your gifts
To where the outlines of waves remain,
Where everything in the wild universe
Can be traced to its ontic source,
So that you in your error and I in mine
May someday be able to join each other
Far from the call of illusion and metal
And the light feet of my dreams can sprout wings
And fly off to greet you on the axis of the one true language.

Aunt Lee Dying, Surrounded by Family

The end came swaying toward you
Over a field of hot llamas thirsting for glacial omens.
We on the other hand found ourselves bent in deference
To, how should I say, "th'artifice of it all,"

The gristle of our allegiance to you.
And which is worse, the malleable fusion
Of our averted eyes, or the piecing together of ceremony,
"The merest husk of faith,"

Such as measuring the air left in the lungs
Of a raggier self?
I keep losing what I'm trying to say.
Or, we must listen to the voices that seem useless:

The colorful nuzzling of a trumpet
Against the necks of lions and lambs.
In other words, my hands are grafted to lamentation
And two occult, adamantine wings gleam behind me

Hooked onto the lineaments of pride scowling across the lilting scene.
In fact, the whole place is gravid with language
Dressed in a paper gown
In which you are patted on the back from all directions.

Now the nightfall is an innuendo risen from the dark roots of afternoon,
And your eyeball vaults across my childhood caked with cake
Spilling a trickle of voices that ultimately bow,
This being the bad taste with which we apprenticed ourselves to your ways.

The Number 4 Comforts a Sad Child

The chiasmic beat of your feet
Flies from the world contracting
Around you, a world where
Only the cockroaches in the bathtub keep
Keeping. I am the Father,
I am the Son and I am
Especially the Holy Ghost and I am
Also something more, how can I say?—
Stable—than they who haunt you
In a triptych of blue on your wall
Every night before you sleep.
I am the memories of tomorrow keeping
You tied to the clockhands by a string
That lets you billow out for awhile
And look at it all and look
At it all to remember it only
In the last few seconds of a dream
Where you hear me in some imagined rain
Like the windshield wiper of a bus:
ur-ur ur-ur   ur-ur ur-ur
Calling to you, calling,
And though you don't yet know it,
My child, pulling you absolutely through.

Sestina for Lizzette

I've always wanted to write a poem about San Francisco,
But I was only there once, and on my honeymoon
No less, and to tell the truth, it sucked.
No, not because I had supposedly just sold my soul
For heterosexual privilege (which, ironically
Enough, I'd had much more of with you, what with your decent parents,

Unlike someone else's parents
Who I am forbidden by law to mention in a poem). San Francisco
Just *felt* bad to me, even with City Lights and all, Michel Foucault ironic
In his kimono, peering from the mirrored cover of his recent honeymoon
With that foppish, prurient, straight-as-an-arrow soul
Of an American professor. The year was 1992, and I was a sucker

For anything purple. Even my wedding dress was as purple as a well-sucked
Patch of neck a teenager tries to hide from the parents
With a bandanna or a flimsy scarf. In my soul
I knew I was still holding onto our flaccid dream of San Francisco,
Of being honeymoonless
Lesbians together, you the Southern and sinewy and sweetly unironic

Muse of my desires, and I the ironical
Expatriate Jew lovingly sucking
The rest of the poison from the macabre remains of the honeymoon
Of signifier and signified. And both sets of parents
Wholeheartedly approved. But in all the San Franciscoes
We could conjure in our souls,

Always there was the debris left perhaps by the quake of chiding souls
In the intermediate world, or by some ironic
Sandman reminding us that we were still asleep. San Francisco
Fantasy aside, you have to admit we sucked
As a couple, and weren't able to get anywhere near the havoc our parents
Had unintentionally and intentionally wreaked. The honeymoon

Was over for us long before it began. Yet it was this honeymoon
That kept and still may keep my sad and blue-eyed soul
Alive, "a simple garden with acres of sky," and the dream of being parents
Together, you and I, which ironically
Will never happen for me now, as it will take a lifetime to suckle
All the drowned and murdered infants who live in him and me, still
      cradled by a hell worse than my worst projections of San Francisco.

I don't understand it when parents say ironic
Things about their children. It seems an extended honeymoon of souls
Sucked through an oblivion of bad land. Good-bye Mom, Dad.
      Good-bye San Francisco.

Note

*The "American professor" at the end of stanza two is James Miller,
who wrote the biography* The Passion of Michel Foucault.

III

We are the mimics. Clouds are pedagogues.
The air is not a mirror but bare board,
Coulisse bright-dark, tragic chiaroscuro

And comic color of the rose, in which
Abysmal instruments make sounds like pips
Of the sweeping meanings that we add to them.

—Wallace Stevens

Le Marteau sans maitre

after Boulez

The winds are blessed today with a new intonation,
Although most of our views through windows
Are implied, rather than explicitly recorded.
In this way, our reactions to the written word

Open an angle of view increasingly peopled
By our club-shaped shadows,
And by our footprints on the road which lie
In an allegorically restrained

Framework of geometric shapes, as elegantly austere
As the simple arrangement of vessels on a table.
Always, those signs dance on the margin
Of the intelligence of a soul. And, most of the time,

They mark the distance between the white reserve
Of a blank expanse of wall, and the pigment blended
From the dust of crushed pearls then splashed
Across the tradition of pure hues, straight from the tube.

It is an honor, really, rather than a sign
Of neglect, when the wine-colored light from a calm sea
In summer bounces off the surface of a clear thought.
The gift, we think, is the reconstruction of data

In a mirror with three wings, each representing
The reflection of unattainable things we still want,
E.g., the quiet absorption of an aging physique,
A map to the furthest limit that we can still imagine,

Though vaguely, the never-ending stimulus of candlelight
Flickering off the lovely one's sleeves...
The gift in fact is the savage pier-walk,
The gift is something that falls dramatically

From the naked eyes traveling in sleep
Along frantic roads. Accept it:
There is a new intonation.
The winds are blessed, the water,

And everything is bound up in chains
Of the expected unexpected, the delirium
In the symbolic center of hazy light.
And our vantage point is unusual,

And it welcomes us into the dark foreground
Which anchors our reflections
To the physical presence of the city,
Whether it is to the rough stone of a bridge,

The brick or mortar of walls,
Or the rippling of tiles. So you see, the scene
Is quite human after all, a liquid legend
Passing through crystalline sunlight

And flooding our well-supported interiors
With an atmospheric clarity emblematic
Of the essential questions blowing here and there
Like remnants of a forgotten language,

Bits of metal riding on a stream of milk
That, virginal, will never cease to flow,
And yet they will haunt us like the glowing flecks
Rising from a book's crumpled cover, burning.

What I Want to Tell You but Can't

The night is a river of violence.
The night is awash with license plates
Jammed into the backsides of shark-like cars.
And the blackened jungle of my offshore longings

Is raked through with starlight
Where some terror is exhaled.
A creature sealed in deepest amber,
I have grown immune to horizons

Dragging their bars of leaden sunlight
Against a destiny wrapped
Around me like a fence
That I will never climb,

Rippling in time with the savage cracking
Of a sheet pinned to whitest wind.
Come morning, I must face that these words
Will be worth nothing, as the trees,

Disarmed by night's startling opacity,
Will have fully shed their bitter gloamings.
But what is this that keeps me
From balling up, a wet sweater

Spun into a skein whose shrunken diameter
I would surely take in stride? From now on,
I fear that I must sleep on one side,
Violated by a laughing weapon in a dream,

And wake to the death clamped to various eyelashes
Pouring through the subway doors,
Still peddling my pretext of wilted joy
Like rainy flowers on the street.

I have already thrown the proof
For this poem into the flames.

Having a Job

Necessities rain down like anvils.
And all the bothersome triumphs
Come slamming at my jaded window
Streaked with afternoon's thick demands.

This morning I saw a woman so confident
She put her belongings in a see-
Through bag, picked her hair
With impunity on the crowded train.

It's got a great feel to it,
Someone said to someone else,
While I stood there, shuffling
In and out of the light

Of the burgeoning sun,
Largely out of focus.
It's not worth the time it takes
To peel an orange, I thought,

To watch stockings wrinkling bitterly
Around pinched ankles, my own in particular.
But to ignore is to respect sometimes,
And the powdery blue sheen

Of liabilities splattered across my eyelids
Actually helps, as the early morning
Does its foggy steamroll over the leaves
That catch in misty asphalt cracks.

And then there is the provocative wash
Of Saturdays, the Tuesday as green
As a summer leaf. It is beautiful,
Really, when rains harden

Into sidewalks, when sidewalks
Glimmer into winter, and the fumes
From various people cease to regulate
The propinquity of admiring eyes.

Yet this lifetime propels us to further
Intuitions, and epic elegies
Do not make much sense anymore,
At least not to me, scrambling around

Like a giant fly seduced into the vile
Metaphysics tangled among the slats
Of a ceiling fan churning the syrupy light
Of all worthwhile desire.

Yet I realize these things I've seen
Dissolving into spots before my eyes
Are the things legends are made of,
But don't expect me to believe a word of it,

Not now, and with one last gasp
Into an age's anarchic gyre,
My face blues over this era
That has birthed and murdered me.

In Spring

I saw you standing outside the station,
And the two plus two of our charcoal eyes
Traveled up my chilly spine's rebuke,
So close that I could taste the fibers

In the lining of your coat,
Paradisal in its drizzled taunt.
I wanted to say, lie down with me
Inside the warm coil of boulevards between us,

Rhythmic as the sulphur light that laps the hubcaps.
We could exchange recipes for astonishing a dune
While the sweat rolled off us in oceans of pure soul,
And I would sing my unmediated feral song

Into the seashell of your darkest dream.
But something else lodged in my throat—
A sin for all time that cackles
At its own serrated mewling.

Who'd have guessed I'd be so silent
As you cocked your priestly head—
I wonder, did you even recognize me?
Since then I've fiddled with a blueprint

For a room filled only with the smell of you.
The mornings shed their circles at my feet
And...and what? No sign of you, of course.
But I saw you standing outside the station,

And the two plus two of our charcoal eyes
Traveled up my chilly spine's rebuke,
So close that I could taste the fibers
In the lining of your coat, so very close.

Autobiography

How poor I step into form,
Step into infinity, how poor a wrought-iron cross.
To slip on the sweat of a tendon,

How poor the yearning in the pause
Before the embrace, to taste the nothing
In the morning streets. Because

When veins are threaded with the splintering
Of solid doves made out of bone,
I ration my comings and goings

But the hero always returns home.
The ink extracted from a comet
Gives me something to own,

Yet this illusion seems to plummet
Without benefit of a fiery tail
Or hand that passes through blankets

Of thick thick flame. Meanwhile, the rails
Of Why create (destroy) my alibi
As I endure blindly, count my steps as I inhale.

Blood Brother

You came to me just like that,
A quasi-lunar jukebox booming
The smoky burden of all I have not said,
The premonitions once clasped

Inside a dusk-animal's gravelly voice.
You know, the ones about the evil mimes
That stand for something,
The hand extended to the fair recesses of exits

And then the footbridge doused with kerosene...
If I pretend that none of this concerns me,
I do it because I admire the way the air softens
When you waft into a room

At the exact moment of an accident,
The way sapphires bow to your open eyes
That snag on their desires,
And the way the wind just sort of sidles up to you

And shifts the plaid odyssey of hair across your neck.
If I walk away, do you think the saddles
Of my shoes will not rise up
And claim the ferocity of muffled light

Soldered to the nails deepening beneath them?
Or that those very nails will not snap themselves in protest
Against the narcolepsy that seems to smite
Whole towns sizzling with buoyant coffins

No alphabet can contain?
Will I be forgiven if I do not thrust my tongue
Into the damp cocoon fastened

To your bewildered chimney full of spirits
Casting off its slender wiles where flames used to be?

Repeat After Me

We couldn't help but make careers out of it,
The saccharine familiarity with which you greeted
Us. I feel like writing this in a French you will pretend
To understand but won't, to render, for instance, the verb
"Gagner" which means in French "to win"
"Reveiller" (to wake up), to revel in the disdain

With which you throw your flowers at our feet, the disdain
With which we let you. It
Is a terrible thing indeed to win
The spoils of the condemned, like greeting
A deaf person in the dark, a vague presumption of verbs
Continued by other means. Oh, I guess it helps that you pretend

An interest in what we ourselves pretend
An interest in, all the while disdaining
Those long filaments of grief that you hold out for us to touch. Sometimes
    we even turn to useless verbs,
"Who can say what it means or whether it
Protects?" The cruel union of magpies greets
Us daily now, incites the urge to win

Those sandbags of narcissism, which is the same as winning
Sandbags of immortality used to be, do you understand? Pretend
For one moment that you are me. Does it embarrass you to greet
Yourself this way, do you disdain
This kind of play, would you ignore it
If you could bring yourself to see into the meaning of the verb

"To ignore" with the fury with which you have ignored the verb
"To be"? Or is it that no one can win
In general anymore, is it
That when any one of us invents a pretext
To hurl our lonely jeremiads, they echo only the disdain
With which we choose to greet

The Other, that poignant deviation that greets
Us in the mirror of some passive verb:
"When all has been said and done, I find myself disdained
And I adore it. Yet I have no wish to win
At anything per se, and this is why I am left standing, as The Pretenders
Say, 'in the middle of the road,' the road itself

A symbol of the disdain I encounter upon winning
Your greeting which implies the verb
'Gagner' and the pretense under which you offer it"?

A Losing War

This blue medal dangling from my chest
Betokens something shifting deep inside me:
The lone geometry of hangers whispering
In a closet, the string swaying

Like viscous spittle from its naked bulb.
I feel the onset of a lifelong habit,
Heresy perhaps, along with the sad arrogance
Of some self-incarceration.

A hasty decision is at hand, in any case.
But the torn aroma of the fog
Is what I'm after, the flight of phantom wind
From underneath a serenade of arrows

Emblazoned with the broken sneer
Of syllables smeared across the ages.
And if the shadows buried
In the air began to rasp,

The scarred viscera of rescue
Would hurl themselves across the carpet,
And surely they would find me in my barracks
A million miles away from polite society.

Hindsight Is Always Best

I hiccup all the time without you,
Drifting from birdhouse to birdhouse,
A body bag left smiling across my upended wall.
It will take more than an ionosphere of fizzled blindness

To knock me out of my rowdy daydream,
More than any unsubstantiated neural howl
Turning solid in the morning air
Like a brittle hunk of suffering or trust.

I know that only the spangled soul
Of a lilac that goes on tingling forever
(In the force field of my dependency,
In the forfeiture of my depravity)

Will be able to embrace the somnolence
That shrouds the painted refrain of baseball bats
Sold for an outrageous amount at some exhibit
Where, by the way, I *was* drunk,

Because I couldn't help it, or simply didn't care, etc.
"No one in their right mind would laugh
At such a thing," someone hissed
In my direction over the telegram flourishing

Its morbid news into the room,
But I could tell it was a cipher begging for relief,
And besides, I felt so safe there as you clinked
Away your own diversions in your livid glass.

As for the question of the body bag—
"Only a prank," I assured the gawking neighbors
Later on that night through handcuffs,
"Ladies and gentlemen, only a prank."

The Passion According to G.H.

after Clarice Lispector

The night cuts across us like a vibrating pin
And we dissolve into our private eyesores
As snowflakes on a great, lolling tongue

Bleating from a far-off, far-off fog. More
Like St. Paul than not, we are crafty
And full of certainty. Like him, we make our

Own Damascus. This is why I still carry
My suitcase, shot through with ultimatums
And wedded to fissures of starlight and empty.

Yet I live in a violent world and I am in love
Lemonade, everything was so infinite
While colorless green ideas sleep furiously on.

So be still my molten heartstrings;
I will continue my song.
I will continue my song in the name of nothing

But a glittering metastasis that hatches a chitin moon
Into a blood tide—a lighted, fuzzy, six-legged thing
That bears and bears alone.

What I Mean When I Say I'm a Poet

I found my life lying in the ruins
Of a pop-out book of some city.
I rummaged through the garbage pails
For fallen stars while streetlamps

Seared my breath, chewed gray paint
Curling from walls until forgetfulness rustled
Like the blank applause of summer leaves,
And I fell asleep in a library of lead.

Outside you shivered on a bench,
Until a bullet from the moon
Splintered it into pieces and you were
The alphabet personified,

Words echoing alchemical sands
Shifting beneath the Sphinx,
A discovery of iridescence in the images
Of ancient books while the motors

Of terrestrial habits revved past
Your parabolic exile with their golden
Batteries of sunlight.
I often wonder if I will awake

To a new day gleaming on its empty plate,
Trembling in the web of dull grace
Weaving its way toward me in that attic-
Space after a dream which leaves

An impression burned onto a screen
Like the one lit up before me now,
A fragile winnowing of thoughts
Where I find I am the clothes of my own illusion,

A coat hung from a point of light
On one of history's dark maneuvers.
Meanwhile your blood flows
In time with the rivers.

The places where you once walked
Smell of the shade.

While Writing

Someone inside says, "Get busy."
But I've got appointments to keep,
I have an abstemious love of equations calculated quickly
While the tepid day melts into design.

And the high cheekbones of the beautiful life
Bear the loose look of a calendar by lamplight.
I search for patterns in everything.
I am tied in knots of comprehension.

I think, how useful it might be
To pierce all the hands of the earth
With an oath of pins encircling snarling planets.
But talent and shallowness sewn together

Is nothing but a kerchief tied around a survivalist's head,
And it helps to know the feet wriggling through a hole
In the universe will land for an instant
Upon the cushions of the dark,

And that after marching one doozy of a kilometer after another,
We each come upon the same poem scribbled in invisible ink
Taped to the door of a room
In which an austere justice is burning for us.

The Laugh of the Medusa

after Hélène Cixous

The eternal feminine has been argued
Right out of existence, and so we produce
That which is not us: a leaf falling
Through whiteness, a veil veiling the absolute virility
Of all motion. And every truth is a scandal,
And every truth is nothing but the rain

Battering the window of thought like a bunch of sticks, the rain
Without the window, the window without any argument
Whatsoever to provoke scandal.
The leafy green produce,
The lettuce, the okra, and even the asparagus lose their virility
In the face of this crisis, falling

From grace and innocence like the gardeners of the original Fall.
Nothing, not even whole seas, let alone a little rain,
Will swell these vegetables to their former virility
(Although in some circles it is argued
That any attempt to artificially produce
Such an effect in the first place is to scandalize

Their Maker, Who is believed to be beyond scandal
In others). The question, then, is if we have in fact fallen,
What more can we do than assist in the production
Of nature as we perceive it? For instance, the wild rain
On the shutters of an old, sad house full of the arguments
Of angry baby-boomers discontented with their childrens' unvirile

Pursuits; i.e., their sallow brands of the virile
(Some would say "castrated") version of what would have created a scandal
In their own long-lost heyday. "All these kids are good for is arguing
And lying around like ripened fruit ready to fall
Off a tree, having soaked up gallons of rain
So that their only hope is to become produce,

And with that unlofty goal, they will assist in the production
Of nothing except a kind of brute, gravitational virility.
A silent, telescopic reign
Of terror, is what it is!" This, and many other scandals
Have said their prayers and fallen
Asleep in the wake of half-drunken argument.

The rain falls
Up. Production ceases. Monique still argues
Loudly with Hélène: "Ceci est une scandale! Vive la virilité!"

Note

"Monique" is Monique Wittig, the French feminist theorist.

Noelle Kocot was born and raised in Brooklyn, New York. She holds a B.A. from Oberlin College and an M.F.A. from the University of Florida, and was awarded a fellowship from the National Endowment for the Arts for 2001. Noelle currently lives with her husband in the Midwood section of Brooklyn.

Funding for the 1999 Levis Poetry Prize was provided in part by a generous donation in memory of John J. Wilson.